T0127450

CHILLIES

CHILLIES

A BOOK OF RECIPES

HELEN SUDELL

LORENZ BOOKS

First published in 2013 by Lorenz Books
an imprint of Anness Publishing Limited
Blaby Road, Wigston, Leicestershire LE18 4SE
www.annesspublishing.com
www.lorenzbooks.com
info@anness.com

If you like the images in this book and would like to investigate using them for publishing, promotions or advertising, please visit our website www.practicalpictures.com for more information

A CIP catalogue record for this book is available from
The British Library

Publisher Joanna Lorenz
Editorial Director Helen Sudell
Designer Nigel Partridge
Illustrations Anna Koska

Photographers: Martin Brigdale, Nicki Dowey, Steve Moss,
  William Lingwood, Craig Robertson, Charlie Richards, Gus Filgate,
  Simon Smith
Recipes by: Ghillie Basan, Jenny White, Joanna Farrow, Pepita Aris,
  Maxine Clark, Matthew Drennan, Sallie Morris, Alex Barker,
  Carol Pastor, Sunil Vijayakar, Terry Tan, Young Jin Song, Lucy Knox,
  Jane Milton

Printed and bound in China

COOK'S NOTES

• Bracketed terms are intended for American readers.

• For all recipes, quantities are given in both metric and imperial measures and, where appropriate, in standard cups and spoons. Follow one set of measures, but not a mixture, because they are not interchangeable.

• Standard spoon and cup measures are level. 1 tsp = 5ml, 1 tbsp = 15ml, 1 cup = 250ml/8fl oz.

• Australian standard tablespoons are 20ml. Australian readers should use 3 tsp in place of 1 tbsp for measuring small quantities.

• American pints are 16fl oz/2 cups. American readers should use 20fl oz/2.5 cups in place of 1 pint when measuring liquids.

• Electric oven temperatures in this book are for conventional ovens. When using a fan oven, the temperature will probably need to be reduced by about 10–20°C/20–40°F. Since ovens vary, you should check with your manufacturer's instruction book for guidance.

• The nutritional analysis given for each recipe is calculated per portion (i.e. serving or item), unless otherwise stated. If the recipe gives a range, such as Serves 4–6, then the nutritional analysis will be for the smaller portion size, i.e. 6 servings. The analysis does not include optional ingredients, such as salt added to taste.

• Medium (US large) eggs are used unless otherwise stated.

PUBLISHER'S NOTE

CONTENTS

INTRODUCTION

Powerhouses of flavour and fire, chillies are wonderful to cook with, and are well worth exploring in all their many and varied forms. Their reputation as one of the hottest properties on the culinary scene is undoubtedly well deserved, but what is equally true is that they can also be subtle. Add a whole chilli when cooking a casserole or stew, remove it at the end, and you introduce the merest flicker of flame. To turn up the heat a little bit, use sliced

Below: These small Thai chillies pack an incredible punch.

medium-hot chillies, defusing them somewhat by scraping out the seeds. Later, if your courage (and your constitution) will stand it, go for the burn by cooking with the hottest varieties, leaving the seeds in.

Chillies are native to Central and Southern America and were a well-kept secret for centuries. When Spanish conquistadors arrived in the sixteenth century, they were struck by how delicious the local food was, and gold was not the only treasure they took with them when they sailed for home. Europeans embraced chillies with great enthusiasm, and within a short time they had also been introduced to Asia.

COOKING WITH CHILLIES

Chillies add their distinctive flavour to dishes as diverse as Indian, Malaysian and Thai curries, Hungarian goulash and Austrian paprika schnitzel. In

Above: Chilli powder adds heat in an instant.

France, rouille, that innocent-looking red mayonnaise that accompanies bouillabaisse is spiked with chillies.

Mexico continues to furnish some of the most exciting and innovative chilli recipes. With so many varieties at their disposal, Mexican cooks will often use two types of chilli in the same recipe, one selected for its pungency, perhaps; another to add a hint of sweetness.

For years, the only chillies in our markets and supermarkets

were the slim tapered red and green serranos or cayennes. However, travellers titillated by the tastes of spicy dishes in other countries have prompted a demand for a wider range of chillies. We can now get to know this exciting ingredient better, not only in its fresh form, but also dried, and in sauces, salsas and pickles.

GROWING AND HARVESTING CHILLIES

If you can grow tomatoes, then you should succeed with chillies as they prefer similar

Below: Grow chillies in pots in a sunny position.

conditions. You can grow them in tubs, hanging baskets or pots on the windowsill. Raise the plants under glass in spring, or buy them from a good plant nursery. Plant out when frost is no longer a problem and the first flowers are visible. Water well in dry weather, mulch and feed fortnightly with a high-potash fertilizer. Pinch out growing tips if sideshoots are not being made and stop once they have set fruit.

Harvest about 12–16 weeks after planting out. Pull up the plants and hang under glass in a sunny place when frost threatens to encourage the fruit to continue ripening.

STORING CHILLIES

The best way to store fresh chillies is to wrap them well in kitchen paper, place them in a plastic bag and keep them in the chiller compartment of the refrigerator. They will keep well for a week or more but it is a good idea to check them occasionally and discard any

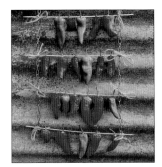

Above: Hang chillies up to dry in a well-ventilated area.

that begin to soften. Chillies can also be frozen. There is no need to blanch them if you plan to use them fairly quickly.

Store ground chillies in airtight jars in a cool place out of direct sunlight. Buy small quantities and use as soon as possible. Some cooks store dried chillies in the freezer.

To dry your own fresh chillies thread them on a string, hang them in a warm, dry place until they are crumbly, then use a pestle to crush them in a mortar. Store in a sterilized jar out of direct sunlight.

TYPES OF CHILLI

ANAHEIM
These large Mexican chillies are mild to medium hot. The skin can be a little tough so they are best roasted and peeled. They can also be stuffed or used in sauces, stews and salsas.

JALAPEÑO
Available green or red, fresh or pickled, jalapeños are hot and are used in tamales, salsas and sauces. They are freely available in supermarkets.

HABANERO
Also known as Scotch Bonnet, these chillies are extremely hot. They are used in Caribbean jerk sauces.

CHIPOTLE
The dried, smoked versions of jalapeño chillies, chipotle chillies give an intense heat to soups or stews. Chipotles need long, slow cooking to soften them and bring out their full flavour, which is hot and smoky.

THAI
These tiny chillies are fairly hot and are used in salads and in Thai curry paste.

ANCHO
These are dried and are mild and sweet. After rehydration, anchos can be stuffed, and they also taste great sliced or chopped in stirfries.

CASCABEL
The name translates as 'little rattle', and refers to the sound the seeds make inside this round dried chilli. Cascabels are great in stews, soups and salsas.

GUAJILLO
These dried chillies are a deep reddish brown with a smooth texture. Fairly mild in flavour, and very good with seafood.

TEPIN
Tiny and blisteringly hot, tepin chillies are used to make hot pepper sauce for Thai cuisine.

INDIAN
Small and very hot, so use with caution. They are mostly used in curries and stir-fries.

CAYENNE
There are several varieties of the cayenne chilli, including the popular 'long hot reds'. Cayenne pepper is a pungent spice made from a mixture of blended cayenne chillies.

HOT CHILLI POWDER AND CHILLI FLAKES
Commercially ground powder and flakes are used to spice up sausages, sauces and oils.

MINCED CHILLI, CHILLI OIL AND HOT RED PEPPER SAUCE
Minced chilli is a paste made from ground red chillies. Chilli oil is good for frying, or basting meat or fish on the barbecue. Hot red pepper sauce is very popular in Malaysian and Caribbean cuisine.

Jalapeño

Cayenne

Hot chilli power

Chilli flakes

Anaheim

Habanero

Ancho

Indian

Cascabel

Thai

Guajillo

Tepin

Minced chilli

Chilli oil

Hot red pepper sauce

Chipotle

CHILLI TECHNIQUES

The oil in chillies contains a chemical, capsaicin, which is a strong irritant, so it is vital to handle chillies with care. Work in a well-ventilated area and wear gloves, if possible.

CHOOSING CHILLIES
Fresh chillies should be firm, glossy and evenly coloured. Avoid any musty or soft chillies.

It is a good idea to buy dried chillies in transparent packaging, so that you can see the quality at a glance. If dried chillies look a little dusty when you remove them from the packaging, don't worry, just wipe them gently with a piece of kitchen paper before use.

Chilli flakes and commercially ground chillies should have good aroma and a rich, strong colour. If chilli powder looks quite dark, this is not a sign that it is stale, rather an indication that the chillies have been mixed with other spices, American-style.

CHOPPING CHILLIES
To prepare, slit chillies lengthways with a sharp knife.

Scrape out the seeds. Slice the chillies or chop them finely. Much of the fiery heat is concentrated in the seeds, so you may prefer to discard some or all of them. If you have worked without gloves, wash your hands several times in soapy water. Avoid touching your face, particularly the eye area.

SOAKING DRIED CHILLIES
Most dried chillies must be rehydrated before being used. Put the seeded chillies in a roasting tin (pan) in the oven for a few minutes, or press them on to the surface of a hot, dry, heavy frying pan. Once this is done continue as below.

1 Wipe the chillies to remove any surface dirt. If you like, you can slit them and shake out the seeds before soaking.

2 Put the chillies in a bowl and pour over hot water to cover. If necessary, fit a saucer in the bowl to keep them submerged. Soak for 20–30 minutes, or until the colour is restored and the chillies have softened and swelled in size.

3 Drain the chillies, cut off the stalks if necessary, then slit the and scrape out the seeds. Slice or chop the flesh.

ROASTING FRESH CHILLIES

There are several ways of roasting fresh chillies. You can use the grill, roast them in the oven, dry-fry as explained below, or hold them over a gas flame.

1 Put the chillies in a dry frying pan and place the pan over a medium heat. Turn the chillies over every few minutes until the skins are charred and starting to blister.

2 Slip the roasted chillies into a strong plastic bag and tie the top to keep the steam in. Set aside for 20 minutes. Take the chillies out of the bag and remove the skins, either by peeling them off, or by gently rubbing the chillies with a clean dish towel.

MAKING A CHILLI FLOWER

This makes a very attractive garnish for a special dish.

1 Cut a chilli lengthways from the tip to within 1cm/½ in of the stem end. Remove the seeds. Repeat the lengthways cuts around the chilli.

2 Rinse the chilli in cold water, place in a bowl of iced water and chill for at least 4 hours. For very curly flowers, leave the chilli overnight. When ready to use, lift the chilli out and drain it on kitchen paper.

GRINDING CHILLIES

When making chilli powder, this method gives a distinctive and smoky taste.

1 Soak the chillies, if dried, pat dry and then dry-fry in a heavy pan over a gentle heat until crisp. Transfer to a mortar and grind to a powder with a pestle. Store out of direct sunlight in an airtight container.

'FIRE' EXTINGUISHERS

If you inadvertently chomp on a chilli and feel as though your mouth is on fire, reach for bread, rice, natural yogurt or milk. Whatever you do, avoid sparkling water or any other fizzy drink, as it will just make the problem worse.

BASIC CHILLI RECIPES

CHILLI RELISH

Make this at least an hour before serving to allow the flavours to blend.

Chop 2 large tomatoes finely. Place them in a mixing bowl. Chop 1 red onion and 1 garlic clove. Add to the tomatoes, mix well, then stir in 10ml/1 tsp chilli sauce (use a sweet chilli sauce or a hot one, as you like).
   Stir in 15ml/1 tbsp chopped fresh basil and 1 chopped green chilli – with the seeds if you like a hot relish – then add a pinch each of salt and sugar.

CHILLI AND TOMATO OIL

Heating oil with chillies intensifies the rich flavour. This intense oil tastes great sprinkled on fresh pasta or on top of cooked pizzas.

Heat 150ml/¼ pint/²/₃ cup olive oil in a pan. When it is very hot, but not smoking, stir in 10ml/1 tsp tomato purée (paste) and 15ml/1 tbsp dried red chilli flakes, then leave to cool in the pan.
   Pour into an airtight, sterilized jar and store in the refrigerator for up to 2 months.

HARISSA

This fiery North African sauce is an indispensable store cupboard ingredient for many Moroccan families. For a delicious taste, brush a small amount over chicken wings before grilling (broiling) them.

Remove the seeds from 115g/ 4oz dried red chillies, then soak them in enough warm water to cover them completely until they soften. Drain well. Using scissors, snip the chillies into chunks, then pound them to a paste in a pestle and mortar.

Add 4 chopped garlic cloves, 2.5ml/½ tsp salt, 15ml/1 tbsp ground cumin and 10ml/2 tsp each of dried mint and caraway seeds. Grind to a paste, then stir in 60ml/4 tbsp olive oil. Scrape into a sterilized jar, cover with a layer of olive oil and chill. It can be kept in the refrigerator for up to 6 weeks.

PICKLED CHILLIES

Preserved chillies in vinegar are easy to prepare and endlessly versatile: Chop them up and add to a green salad; serve them alongside a platter of cold meats; or add to a chunky cheese sandwich.

The easiest way to pickle chillies is to slit them, remove the seeds and pack them in sterilized jars with spiced vinegar to cover. Store the jar out of direct sunlight.

Alternatively, cut off the tops, leaving the cores and seeds intact, then slice the chillies in half widthways. Blanch them in a 50:50 mixture of white vinegar and water, with a little salt. Leave it to cool, then pack into sterilized jars, tucking whole peeled garlic cloves between the layers.

Fill the jars with olive oil, close tightly and leave for at least 2 weeks before using.

ROUILLE

Traditionally added to the French fish stew, bouillabaisse, this is a red chilli mayonnaise.

Peel and deseed 1 fresh red chilli, pound to a paste with 2 garlic cloves and scrape the mixture into a bowl. Add 2 egg yolks, 5ml/1 tsp of red pepper mustard and 15ml/1 tbsp lemon juice. Whisk in 2.5ml/½ tsp cayenne pepper.

Have ready 250ml/8fl oz/1 cup of olive oil and of sunflower oil. Whisking constantly, add the oil to the mixture drop by drop, then in a slow stream, until the mixture thickens.

SOUPS AND APPETIZERS

CHILLIES STIMULATE THE APPETITE SO ARE A
PERFECT INGREDIENT TO HELP GET THOSE TASTE
BUDS TINGLING. WHETHER IT IS A WARMING
SOUP OR A SPICY STARTER CHILLIES ARE JUST
WHAT YOU NEED TO BEGIN A MEAL

CUCUMBER AND SALMON SOUP WITH CHILLI SALSA

In this light soup the refreshing flavours of cucumber fuse with the cool salmon and a hint of heat from the salsa to bring the taste of summer to the table.

Serves 4

3 medium cucumbers
300ml/½ pint/1¼ cups Greek yogurt
250ml/8fl oz/1 cup vegetable stock, chilled
120ml/4fl oz/½ cup crème fraîche
15ml/1 tbsp chopped fresh chervil
15ml/1 tbsp snipped fresh chives
15ml/1 tbsp chopped fresh flat leaf parsley
1 small red chilli, seeded and very finely chopped
a little oil, for brushing
225g/8oz salmon fillet, skinned and cut into eight thin slices
salt and ground black pepper
fresh chervil or chives, to garnish

Energy 226kcal/942kj; Protein 3.7g; Carbohydrate 64.1g; of which sugars 64.1g; Fat 16.3g; of which saturates 10.3g; Cholesterol 48mg; Calcium 125mg; Fibre 2.3g; Sodium 280mg.

Peel two of the cucumbers and halve them lengthways. Scoop out and discard the seeds, then roughly chop the flesh. Purée in a food processor or blender, then add the yogurt, stock, crème fraîche, chervil, chives and seasoning, and process until smooth. Chill.

Peel, halve and seed the remaining cucumber. Cut the flesh into small neat dice. Mix with the chopped parsley and chilli. Chill until required.

Brush a griddle or frying pan with oil and heat until very hot. Sear the salmon slices for 1–2 minutes on each side, until tender and charred.

Ladle the chilled soup into soup bowls. Top with two slices of the salmon, then pile a portion of salsa into the centre of each. Garnish with the chervil or chives and serve.

CORN AND RED CHILLI CHOWDER

Sweetcorn and chillies make good bedfellows, and here the cool combination of creamed corn and milk is the perfect foil for the raging heat of the chillies.

Serves 6

2 tomatoes, skinned
1 onion, roughly chopped
375g/13oz can creamed
   sweetcorn
2 red (bell) peppers, halved and
   seeded
15ml/1 tbsp olive oil, plus extra
   for brushing
3 red chillies, seeded and
   chopped
2 garlic cloves, chopped
5ml/1 tsp ground cumin
5ml/1 tsp ground coriander
600ml/1 pint/2½ cups milk
350ml/12fl oz/1½ cups chicken
   stock
3 cobs of corn, kernels removed
450g/1lb potatoes, finely diced
60ml/4 tbsp double (heavy)
   cream
60ml/4 tbsp chopped fresh
   parsley
salt and ground black pepper

Process the tomatoes and onion in a food processor or blender to a smooth purée. Add the creamed sweetcorn and process again, then set aside. Preheat the grill (broiler) to high.

Put the peppers, skin sides up, on a grill rack and brush with oil. Grill (broil) for 8–10 minutes, until the skins blacken and blister. Transfer to a bowl and cover with clear film, then leave to cool. Peel and dice the peppers, then set them aside.

Heat the oil in a large pan and add the chopped chillies and garlic. Cook, stirring, for 2–3 minutes, until softened.

Add the ground cumin and coriander, and cook for a further 1 minute. Stir in the sweetcorn purée and cook for about 8 minutes, stirring occasionally.

Pour in the milk and stock, then stir in the corn kernels, potatoes, red pepper and seasoning to taste. Cook for 15–20 minutes, until the corn and potatoes are tender.

Pour into deep bowls and add the cream, then scatter over the chopped parsley and serve at once.

Energy 294kcal/1347kj; Protein 9.4g; Carbohydrate 43.2g; of which sugars 15.7g; Fat 13.5g; of which saturates 5g; Cholesterol 18mg; Calcium 119mg; Fibre 5g; Sodium 500mg.

GUACAMOLE

One of the best loved Mexican salsas, this blend of creamy avocado, tomatoes, chillies, coriander (cilantro) and lime now appears on tables the world over.

Serves 6–8

4 medium tomatoes
4 ripe avocados, preferably fuerte
juice of 1 lime
½ small onion
2 garlic cloves
small bunch of fresh coriander (cilantro), chopped
3 fresh red fresno chillies
salt
tortilla chips, to serve

Cut a cross in the base of each tomato. Place the tomatoes in a heatproof bowl and pour over boiling water to cover.

Leave the tomatoes in the water for 3 minutes, then lift them out using a slotted spoon and plunge them into a bowl of cold water. Drain. The skins will have begun to peel back from the crosses. Remove the skins completely. Cut the tomatoes in half, remove the seeds with a teaspoon, then chop the flesh roughly and set it aside.

Cut the avocados in half then remove the stones. Scoop the flesh out of the shells and place it in a food processor or blender. Process until almost smooth, then scrape into a bowl and stir in the lime juice.

Chop the onion finely, then crush the garlic. Add both to the avocado and mix well. Stir in the coriander.

Remove the stalks from the chillies, slit them and scrape out the seeds with a small sharp knife. Chop the chillies finely and add them to the avocado mixture, with the chopped tomatoes. Mix well.

Check the seasoning and add salt to taste. Cover closely with clear film or a tight-fitting lid and chill for 1 hour before serving as a dip with tortilla chips. If it is well covered, guacamole will keep in the refrigerator for 2–3 days.

Energy 108kcal/445kJ; Protein 1.6g; Carbohydrate 3.1g, of which sugars 2.3g; Fat 9.9g, of which saturates 2.1g; Cholesterol 0mg; Calcium 13mg; Fibre 2.3g; Sodium 8mg

COOK'S TIP
Smooth-skinned fuerte avocados are native to Mexico, so would be ideal for this dip. If they are not available, use any avocados, but make sure they are ripe. To test, gently press the top of the avocado; it should give a little.

HOT THAI OMELETTE ROLLS

These tasty egg rolls are made from wedges of a rolled Thai-flavoured omelette. They are frequently served as finger food from the many street stalls in Thai cities.

Serves 2

3 eggs, beaten
15ml/1 tbsp soy sauce
1 bunch garlic chives, thinly
    sliced
1–2 small fresh red or green
    chillies, seeded and finely
    chopped
small bunch fresh coriander
    (cilantro), chopped
pinch of sugar
salt and ground black pepper
15ml/1 tbsp groundnut
    (peanut) oil

For the dipping sauce

60ml/4 tbsp light soy sauce
fresh lime juice, to taste

Energy 189kcal/780kJ; Protein 11.5g;
Carbohydrate 1g, of which sugars 0.9g;
Fat 15.3g, of which saturates 3.9g;
Cholesterol 331mg; Calcium 76mg;
Fibre 0.7g; Sodium 660mg

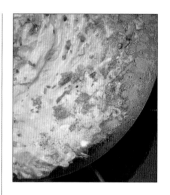

Make the dipping sauce. Pour the soy sauce into a bowl. Add a generous squeeze of lime juice. Taste and add more lime juice if needed.

For the rolls, mix together the beaten eggs, soy sauce, chives, chillies and coriander until well combined. Add the sugar and season to taste. Heat the oil in a large frying pan, pour in the egg mixture and swirl the pan until the mixture evenly coats the base of the pan.

Cook for 1–2 minutes, until the omelette is just firm and the underside is golden. Slide it out on to a plate and roll up as though it were a pancake. Leave to cool completely.

When the omelette is cool, slice it diagonally in 2.5cm/1 in pieces. Arrange the slices on a serving platter and serve with the bowl of dipping sauce.

CHILLI CHEESE MUFFINS

Prepare for a whole new taste sensation with these fabulous spicy muffins. Sharp cheese, aromatic garlic and the hot chilli purée combine in a muffin that is light but filling, with a grainy texture.

Makes 12 standard muffins

115g/4oz/1 cup self-raising (self-rising) flour
15ml/1 tbsp baking powder
225g/8oz/2 cups fine cornmeal (polenta)
150g/5oz/1¼ cups grated mature (sharp) Cheddar cheese
50g/2oz/¼ cup butter, melted
2 eggs, beaten
5ml/1 tsp chilli purée (paste)
1 garlic clove, crushed
300ml/½ pint/1¼ cups milk

Energy 166kcal/698kJ; Protein 5.1g;
Carbohydrate 19.3g, of which sugars 4.4g;
Fat 8.1g, of which saturates 4.6g;
Cholesterol 60mg; Calcium 93mg;
Fibre 0.6g; Sodium 96mg.

Preheat the oven to 200°C/400°F/Gas 6. Line the cups of a muffin tin (pan) with paper cases.

Sift the flour and baking powder together into a large bowl, then stir in the cornmeal and 115g/4oz/1 cup of the grated cheese until well mixed.

In a small bowl, stir together the melted butter, eggs, chilli purée, crushed garlic and milk until thoroughly combined.

Pour the liquid on to the dry ingredients and mix quickly until just combined.

Spoon the batter into the prepared paper cases and sprinkle the remaining grated cheese on top.

Bake for approximately 20 minutes, until risen and golden. Leave to cool for a few minutes before transferring to a wire rack to go cold, or serve warm.

FISH AND SEAFOOD

ADD A LITTLE SPICE TO DELICATE WHITE FISH TO

ENLIVEN THE WHOLE EXPERIENCE. OILIER FISH

AND SHELLFISH ARE MORE ROBUST IN FLAVOUR

SO CHILLIES ARE THE PERFECT ADDITION TO

CREATE A SENSATIONAL MEAL

CHILLI-CRUSTED GOUJONS WITH GUACAMOLE

Small pieces of sole or trout are given a spicy coating, with a hint of chilli, and crisply fried at the table. Serve with a creamy guacamole for a terrific combination of French and Mexican cuisine.

Serves 4–6

450g/1lb sole or pink trout fillets
115g/4oz/1 cup plain (all-purpose) flour
10ml/2 tsp chilli powder
2 eggs, beaten
200g/7oz/3½ cups fresh breadcrumbs
oil, for deep-frying
salt and ground black pepper
4–6 soft wheat tortillas, cut into wedges
Guacamole, to serve (see page 18)
lime wedges, to serve

Energy 275kcal/998kJ; Protein 27g; Carbohydrate 4.1g, of which sugars 0.1g; Fat 14.8g, of which saturates 3.2g; Cholesterol 35mg; Calcium 22mg; Fibre 3g; Sodium 100mg

Cut the fish fillets on the diagonal into pieces about 5mm/¼in thick and 6cm/2½in long. Mix the flour with the chilli powder and salt on a plate. Put the eggs into a shallow bowl. Dip the fish first in the chilli flour, then the egg and finally the breadcrumbs. Place on a serving platter and chill.

Heat the oil in a wok or pan to 190°C/375°F, or test by dropping a cube of day-old bread into the hot oil; it should brown in 30–60 seconds. Place the wok or pan on a burner at the table.

Invite each diner to drop the goujons into the hot oil for 2 minutes, or until golden. Deep-fry the tortilla pieces for a few seconds. Remove with tongs. Eat with the guacamole accompanied by lime wedges for squeezing.

FISH IN CHILLI-SPICED TOMATO SAUCE

This is a traditional Jewish dish. The spiciness of the tomato sauce is refreshing in the sultry heat of the Middle East and is very popular with Israelis. Serve this dish with flat breads and a salad.

Serves 8

300ml/1½ pint/1¼ cups
   passata (bottled strained
   tomatoes)
150ml/¼ pint/²⁄₃ cup fish stock
1 large onion, chopped
60ml/4 tbsp chopped fresh
   coriander (cilantro)
60ml/4 tbsp chopped fresh
   parsley
5–8 garlic cloves, crushed
chopped fresh chilli to taste,
   plus extra for garnishing
large pinch of ground ginger
large pinch of curry powder
1.5ml/¼ tsp ground cumin
1.5ml/¼ tsp ground turmeric
juice of 2 lemons
30ml/1 tbsp vegetable oil
1.fkg/3¼ lb mixed white fish
   fillets
salt and ground black pepper

Put the passata, fish stock, onion, herbs, spices, lemon juice and oil in a pan. Bring the mixture to the boil.

Remove from the heat and add the fish fillets to the hot sauce. Return the pan to the heat and briefly bring the sauce to the boil again. Reduce the heat and simmer very gently for about 5 minutes, or until the fish fillets are all cooked. (Use a fork to test if the fish is tender. If the flesh flakes away easily, then it is cooked.)

Taste the sauce and adjust the seasoning. Serve hot, garnished with chopped chilli.

Energy 191kcal/803kJ; Protein 40.3g; Carbohydrate 18.5g, of which sugars 5.9g; Fat 95.3g, of which saturates 8.9g; Cholesterol 0mg; Calcium 170mg; Fibre 1.7g; Sodium 471mg.

CHILLI PRAWN SKEWERS

Try to get the freshest prawns (shrimp) you can for this recipe. If you buy whole prawns, you will
need to remove the heads and shells, leaving the tail section intact. Serve with extra lime wedges.

Serves 4

16 giant raw prawns (shrimp),
  shelled with the tail section
  left intact
1 lime, cut into 8 wedges
60ml/4 tbsp sweet chilli sauce

Place eight bamboo skewers in cold water and leave to soak for at least 10 minutes, then preheat the grill (broiler) to high.

Thread a prawn on to each skewer, then a lime wedge, then another prawn. Brush the sweet chilli sauce over the prawns and lime wedges.

Arrange the skewers on a baking sheet and grill (broil) for about 2 minutes, turning them once, until cooked through. Serve immediately with more chilli sauce for dipping.

Energy 59kcal/247kJ; Protein 11.13g; Carbohydrate 2.6g, of which sugars 2.5g; Fat 0.40g, of which saturates 0.1g; Cholesterol 122mg; Calcium 61mg; Fibre 0.1g; Sodium 242mg

COOK'S TIP

To shell prawns (shrimp) pull the head from the body, leaving the tail meat intact. Peel off the shell with your fingers leaving the tail flange on. Make a shallow cut along the back of the prawn. Remove the dark intestinal vein that runs along the back.

GRILLED HAKE WITH LEMON AND CHILLI

Choose firm hake fillets, as thick as possible. This is an ideal recipe if you are counting the calories, because it is low in fat. Serve with new potatoes and steamed fine green beans.

Serves 4

4 hake fillets, each 150g/5oz
30ml/2 tbsp olive oil
finely grated rind (zest) and juice
*   of 1 unwaxed lemon*
15ml/1 tbsp crushed chilli flakes
salt and ground black pepper

Preheat the grill (broiler) to high. Brush the hake fillets all over with the olive oil and place them skin side up on a baking sheet.

Grill (broil) the fish for 4–5 minutes, until the skin is crispy, then carefully turn them over using a metal spatula.

Sprinkle the fillets with the lemon rind and chilli flakes and season with salt and ground black pepper.

Grill the fillets for a further 2–3 minutes, or until the hake is cooked through. (Test using the point of a sharp knife; the flesh should flake.) Squeeze over the lemon juice just before serving.

VARIATION

Any firm-fleshed, flaky white fish, such as pollock, haddock or cod would work well in this recipe. Try creamy mashed potatoes with plenty of butter stirred in, if you prefer.

Energy 188kcal/786kJ; Protein 27g; Carbohydrate 0.1g, of which sugars 0.1g; Fat 8.8g, of which saturates 1.2g; Cholesterol 35mg; Calcium 22mg; Fibre 0g; Sodium 150mg

CLAMS WITH CHILLI AND YELLOW BEAN SAUCE

This delicious Thai-inspired dish is simple to prepare. It can be made in a matter of minutes so will not keep you away from your guests for very long.

Serves 4–6
1kg/2¼ lb fresh clams
30ml/2 tbsp vegetable oil
4 garlic cloves, finely chopped
15ml/1 tbsp grated fresh root ginger
4 shallots, finely chopped
30ml/2 tbsp yellow bean sauce
6 red chillies, seeded and chopped
15ml/1 tbsp fish sauce
pinch of sugar
handful of basil leaves, plus extra to garnish

Energy 94kcal/393kJ; Protein 11.6g;
Carbohydrate 2.4g, of which sugars 0.6g;
Fat 4.3g, of which saturates 0.6g;
Cholesterol 45mg; Calcium 75mg;
Fibre 0.7g; Sodium 998mg.

Wash and scrub the clams. Discard any clams that are already open or do not close after tapping them. Heat the oil in a wok or large frying pan. Add the garlic and ginger and fry for about 30 seconds, add the shallots and fry for a further minute.

Add the clams to the pan. Using a fish slice or spatula, turn them a few times to coat all over with the oil. Add the yellow bean sauce and half the chopped red chillies.

Continue to cook, stirring often, for 5–7 minutes, or until all the clams are open. Discard any that do not open at this point. You may need to add a splash of water. Adjust the seasoning with the fish sauce and a little sugar. Finally add the basil leaves and stir to mix.

Transfer the clams to a serving platter. Garnish with the remaining chopped red chillies and basil leaves and serve.

HERB- AND CHILLI-SEARED SCALLOPS ON PAK CHOI

Tender, succulent scallops are simply divine marinated in fresh chilli, fragrant mint and aromatic basil, then quickly seared in a piping hot wok.

Serves 4

20–24 king scallops, cleaned
120ml/4fl oz/½ cup olive oil
finely grated rind (zest) and juice
*   of 1 lemon*
30ml/2 tbsp finely chopped
*   mixed mint and basil*
1 red chilli, seeded and finely
*   chopped*
salt and ground black pepper
500g/1¼lb pak choi (bok choy)

Energy 410kcal/1714kJ; Protein 44.5g;
Carbohydrate 8.3g, of which sugars 2.1g;
Fat 22.3g, of which saturates 3.5g;
Cholesterol 82mg; Calcium 286mg;
Fibre 3.2g; Sodium 494mg

Place the scallops in a shallow, non-metallic bowl in a single layer. In a clean bowl, mix together half the oil, the lemon rind and juice, chopped herbs and chilli and spoon over the scallops. Season well with salt and black pepper, cover and set aside.

Using a sharp knife, cut each pak choi lengthways into four pieces.

Heat a wok over a high heat. When hot, drain the scallops (reserving the marinade) and add to the wok. Cook for 1 minute on each side, or until cooked to your liking.

Pour the marinade over the scallops and remove the wok from the heat. Transfer the scallops and juices to a platter and keep warm.

Wipe out the wok with a piece of kitchen paper and place the wok over a high heat. Add the remaining oil and add the pak choi. Stir-fry for 2–3 minutes, until the leaves are wilted. Divide the greens among four warmed serving plates, then top with the reserved scallops and their juices and serve immediately.

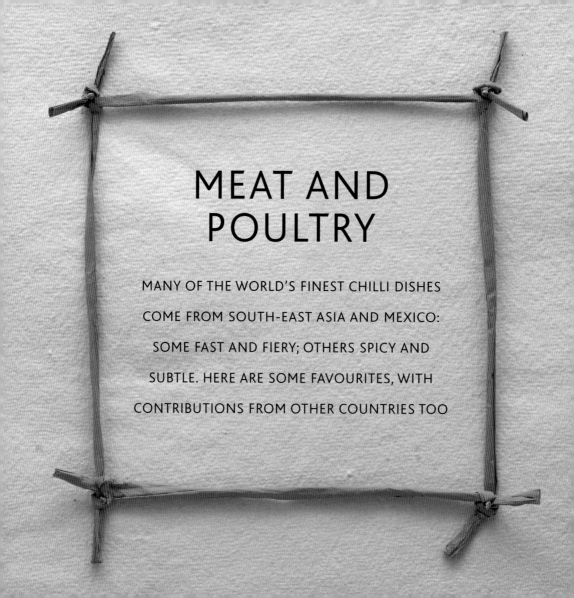

MEAT AND POULTRY

MANY OF THE WORLD'S FINEST CHILLI DISHES
COME FROM SOUTH-EAST ASIA AND MEXICO:
SOME FAST AND FIERY; OTHERS SPICY AND
SUBTLE. HERE ARE SOME FAVOURITES, WITH
CONTRIBUTIONS FROM OTHER COUNTRIES TOO

CHICKEN IN RED SAMBAL

This is a popular dish among Singapore Malays. It is very fiery if you use as many chillies as Malay cooks do. Temper it to your own taste, if you prefer, as less heat does not alter the intrinsic taste.

Serves 4
4 chicken legs
150ml/¼ pint/⅔ cup vegetable or groundnut (peanut) oil
15ml/1 tbsp chilli oil
5ml/1 tsp salt
10ml/2 tsp sugar
4 lime leaves, finely shredded
15ml/1 tbsp tamarind concentrate
200ml/7fl oz/scant 1 cup water

For the spice paste
4–6 dried red chillies, soaked in warm water until soft, squeezed dry and seeded
½ large onion, chopped
4 garlic cloves, chopped
15ml/1 tbsp shrimp paste
4 candlenuts

Energy 290Kcal/1214kJ; Protein 33.5g;
Carbohydrate 3.8g, of which sugars 3.5g;
Fat 15.8g, of which saturates 3.1g;
Cholesterol 123mg; Calcium 58mg;
Fibre 0.2g; Sodium 736mg.

Cut each chicken leg into thigh and drumstick joints and trim off any excess fat. Wash and pat dry.

Heat the oil in a wok or large pan and fry the chicken pieces, turning several times, until the skin is well browned. Lift out with a slotted spoon and set aside. Remove all but 45ml/3 tbsp of the fat.

Grind the ingredients for the spice paste until fine. Fry until fragrant. Add the chilli oil, salt, sugar, lime leaves and tamarind concentrate. Continue to fry for 3 minutes.

Add the chicken and water and simmer for 25–30 minutes, until the chicken is done and the sauce is thick.

CHICKEN WITH CHILLI AND GINGER WINE

The rub for this recipe fuses grated root ginger, warming ginger wine and hot chillies. Their combined flavours infuse the chicken during the steaming process.

Serves 6

1 whole chicken, about
 1.6kg/3½lb
30ml/2 tbsp finely grated fresh
 root ginger
5ml/1 tsp salt
60ml/4 tbsp ginger wine,
 Chinese wine or sherry
5 spring onions (scallions)
2 fresh red chillies

Place the chicken on a deep plate that will fit in your wok or steamer. Put the grated ginger in a bowl and add the salt. Stir in the ginger wine, Chinese wine or sherry. Spread the mixture over the chicken and rub it in well.

Cut the spring onions into 5cm/2in lengths and then into fine strips. Slit the chillies, remove the seeds and thinly slice the flesh. Scatter these evenly over the chicken, with half the spring onion strips.

Place the plate containing the chicken in the steamer or wok. Cover and steam for 1 hour or until it is cooked through, topping up the water in the steamer as necessary.

Carve the chicken and arrange the pieces on a platter. Serve hot or cold, garnished with the remaining spring onion strips.

Energy 394kcal/1634kJ; Protein 33g;
Carbohydrate 0.5g, of which sugars 0.4g;
Fat 27.6g, of which saturates 8g;
Cholesterol 171mg; Calcium 20mg;
Fibre 0.1g; Sodium 136mg.

BARBECUED PORK RIB IN CHILLI SAUCE

Popular as a snack in Korea, these pork ribs are served with green leaves to wrap the meat before eating. The pork is glazed with a sweet and spicy sauce and has a wonderfully charred, smoky taste.

Serves 4

1kg/2¼lb pork ribs
60ml/4 tbsp gochujang *chilli paste*
45ml/3 tbsp Korean chilli powder
30ml/2 tbsp sake or mirin
60ml/4 tbsp sugar
30ml/2 tbsp soy sauce
½ white onion, grated
4 garlic cloves, crushed
7.5ml/1½ tsp grated fresh root ginger
45ml/3 tbsp maple syrup
30ml/2 tbsp sesame oil
salt and ground black pepper
fresh green salad leaves, to serve
sesame seeds, to garnish

Place the pork ribs in a large bowl and pour in enough cold water to cover them, then leave them to soak for about 20 minutes. Drain the ribs and pat dry with kitchen paper.

Remove the bones from the ribs and trim off any excess fat. Slice the meat into 5cm/2in pieces.

Make the marinade. Mix the chilli paste and powder, sake or mirin, sugar, soy sauce, onion, garlic, ginger, maple syrup, sesame oil, salt and pepper in a bowl. Mix well. Add the meat and coat thoroughly with the mixture. Place in the refrigerator and leave it to marinate for at least 3 hours.

Heat a griddle or frying pan over a medium heat and add the pork with the marinade. Cook, turning the pieces once or twice, for 25–30 minutes, until the pork is completely cooked through and the sauce has formed a glaze.

Arrange the pork on salad leaves on a serving plate. Sprinkle with sesame seeds to garnish, and serve.

Energy 638kcal/2663kJ; Protein 49.9g; Carbohydrate 20g, of which sugars 13.8g; Fat 40.8g, of which saturates 14.1g; Cholesterol 165mg; Calcium 83mg; Fibre 1.1g; Sodium 994mg.

LAHORE-STYLE CHILLI LAMB

This hearty dish from Pakistan has a wonderfully pungent flavour imparted by warming chilli and winter spices such as cloves, black peppercorns and cinnamon.

Serves 4
60ml/4 tbsp vegetable oil
1 bay leaf
2 cloves
4 black peppercorns
1 onion, sliced
450g/1lb lean lamb, boned and cubed
1.5ml/¼ tsp ground turmeric
7.5ml/1½ tsp chilli powder
5ml/1 tsp crushed coriander seeds
2.5cm/1in piece cinnamon stick
5ml/1 tsp crushed garlic
7.5ml/1½ tsp salt
1.5 litres/2½ pints/6¼ cups water
50g/2oz/⅓ cup chana dhal or yellow split peas
2 tomatoes, quartered
2 fresh green chillies, thinly sliced

Heat the oil in a wok, karahi or large pan. Lower the heat slightly and add the bay leaf, cloves, peppercorns and onion. Fry for about 5 minutes, or until the onion is golden brown.

Add the cubed lamb, turmeric, chilli powder, coriander seeds, cinnamon stick, garlic and most of the salt, and stir-fry for about 5 minutes over a medium heat.

Pour in 900ml/1½ pints/3¾ cups of the water and cover the pan with a lid or foil, making sure the foil does not come into contact with the food. Simmer for 35–40 minutes or until the lamb is tender.

Put the chana dhal or split peas into a large pan with the remaining measured water and a good pinch of salt and boil for 12–15 minutes, or until the water has almost evaporated and the lentils or peas are soft enough to be mashed. If they are too thick, add up to 150ml/¼ pint/⅔ cup water.

When the lamb is tender, remove the lid or foil and stir-fry the mixture using a wooden spoon, until some free oil begins to appear on the sides of the pan.

Add the cooked lentils to the lamb and mix together well. Stir in the tomatoes and chillies and serve.

Energy 362kcal/1508kJ; Protein 28.6g; Carbohydrate 37.6g, of which sugars 8.0g; Fat 24g, of which saturates 7.3g; Cholesterol 145mg; Calcium 62mg; Fibre 1.6g; Sodium 467mg

CHILLI CON CARNE

Originally made with finely chopped beef, chillies and kidney beans by hungry labourers working on the Texan railroad, this famous Tex-Mex stew has become an international favourite.

Serves 8

1.2kg/2½lb lean braising steak
30ml/2 tbsp sunflower oil
1 large onion, chopped
2 garlic cloves, finely chopped
15ml/1 tbsp flour
300ml/½ pint/1¼ cups red wine
300ml/½ pint/1¼ cups beef stock
30ml/2 tbsp tomato purée (paste)
fresh coriander (cilantro) leaves, to garnish
salt and ground black pepper

For the beans

30ml/2 tbsp olive oil
1 onion, chopped
1 red chilli, seeded and chopped
2 x 400g/14oz cans red kidney beans, drained and rinsed
400g/14oz can tomatoes

For the topping

6 tomatoes, chopped
1 green chilli, chopped
30ml/2 tbsp snipped chives
30ml/2 tbsp coriander (cilantro)
150ml/¼ pint/⅔ cup soured cream

Cut the meat into thick strips and then cut it crossways into small cubes. Heat the oil in a large, flameproof casserole. Add the chopped onion and garlic, and cook until softened but not coloured. Meanwhile, season the flour and place it on a plate, then lightly toss a batch of meat in it.

Use a draining spoon to remove the onion from the pan, then add the floured beef and cook over a high heat until browned on all sides. Remove from the pan and set aside, then flour and brown another batch of meat.

When the last batch of meat is browned, return the first batches with the onion to the pan. Stir in the wine, stock and tomato purée. Bring to the boil, reduce the heat and simmer for 45 minutes, or until the beef is tender.

Meanwhile, for the beans, heat the olive oil in a frying pan and cook the onion and chilli until softened. Add the kidney beans and tomatoes and simmer gently for 20–25 minutes, or until thickened and reduced.

Mix the tomatoes, chilli, chives and coriander for the topping. Ladle the meat mixture on to warmed plates. Add a layer of bean mixture and tomato topping. Finish with soured cream and garnish with chopped coriander leaves. Serve with rice or baked potatoes.

Energy 289kcal/1216kJ; Protein 27.3g; Carbohydrate 24.7g, of which sugars 7.9g; Fat 9.7g, of which saturates 2.8g; Cholesterol 45mg; Calcium 61mg; Fibre 7.8g; Sodium 65mg

MEXICAN CHILLI PIE

Spiced beef is mixed with rice and layered between tortillas and a hot salsa sauce in this fabulous recipe. Perfect for a family meal or to satisfy hungry friends.

Serves 4

1 onion, chopped
2 garlic cloves, crushed
1 red chilli, seeded and sliced
350g/12 oz rump steak, cubed
15ml/1 tbsp vegetable oil
225g/8oz/1 cup cooked rice
beef stock, to moisten
3 large wheat tortillas

For the salsa picante

12 x 400g/14 oz cans tomatoes
2 garlic cloves, halved
1 onion, halved
1–2 fresh red chillies, seeded and roughly chopped
5ml/1 tsp ground cumin
5ml/1 tsp cayenne pepper
salt

For the cheese sauce

50g/2 oz/5 tbsp butter
50g/2 oz/½ cup plain (all-purpose) flour
600ml/1 pint/2½ cups milk
115g/4oz/1 cup grated Cheddar cheese
salt and ground black pepper

Preheat the oven to 180°C/350°F/Gas 4. Make the salsa picante. Place the tomatoes, garlic, onion and chillies in a blender or food processor and process until smooth. Pour into a small pan, add the spices and season with salt. Bring to the boil, stirring occasionally. Boil for 1–2 minutes, then cover and simmer for 15 minutes.

Make the cheese sauce. Melt the butter and stir in the flour. Cook for 1 minute. Add the milk and cook until the sauce thickens. Stir in all but 30ml/2 tbsp of the cheese and season. Set aside.

Mix the onion, garlic and chilli in a bowl. Add the beef and mix well. Heat the oil in a frying pan and stir-fry the mixture for 10 minutes. Stir in the rice and beef stock to moisten. Season to taste.

Pour a quarter of the cheese sauce into an ovenproof dish. Add a tortilla. Spread over half the salsa, then half the meat. Repeat these layers, then add half the remaining cheese sauce and the last tortilla. Pour over the last of the sauce and sprinkle the reserved cheese on top. Bake for 15–20 minutes until golden.

Energy 595kcal/2516kJ; Protein 30.3g; Carbohydrate 91.2g, of which sugars 11.3g; Fat 14.7g, of which saturates 4.7g; Cholesterol 53mg; Calcium 153mg; Fibre 4.0g; Sodium 379mg.

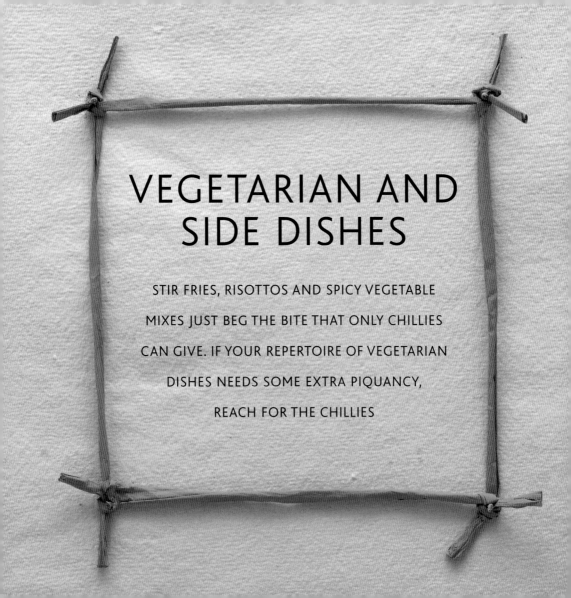

VEGETARIAN AND SIDE DISHES

STIR FRIES, RISOTTOS AND SPICY VEGETABLE

MIXES JUST BEG THE BITE THAT ONLY CHILLIES

CAN GIVE. IF YOUR REPERTOIRE OF VEGETARIAN

DISHES NEEDS SOME EXTRA PIQUANCY,

REACH FOR THE CHILLIES

BROCCOLI AND CHILLI SPAGHETTI

The contrast between the hot chilli and the mild broccoli is delicious in this dish. To add extra flavour, sprinkle the spaghetti and broccoli with grated Parmesan cheese before serving.

Serves 4

350g/12oz dried spaghetti
450g/1lb sprouting broccoli,
    cut into small florets, plus
    leaves
50ml/¼ pint/⅔ cup
    garlic-infused olive oil
1 fat red chilli, seeded and finely
    chopped
1 salt and ground black pepper

Bring a large pan of lightly salted water to the boil. Add the spaghetti and broccoli and cook for 8–10 minutes, until both are tender. Drain thoroughly.

Using the back of a fork crush the broccoli roughly, taking care not to mash the spaghetti strands at the same time.

Meanwhile, warm the oil and finely chopped chilli in a small pan over a low heat and cook very gently for 5 minutes.

Pour the chilli and oil over the spaghetti and broccoli and toss together to combine. Season to taste. Divide between four warmed bowls and serve immediately.

Energy 396kcal/1678kJ; Protein 17.3g;
Carbohydrate 68.3g, of which sugars 6g;
Fat 7.9g, of which saturates 0.8g;
Cholesterol 0mg; Calcium 114mg;
Fibre 5.6g; Sodium 24mg.

PUMPKIN, ROSEMARY AND CHILLI RISOTTO

A dangerously rich and creamy risotto. The pumpkin gradually disintegrates to speckle the rice with orange. The rosemary gives it a sweet pungency, while garlic and chilli add bite.

Serves 4

115g/4oz/½ cup butter
1 small onion, finely chopped
2 large garlic cloves, crushed
1 fresh red chilli, seeded and finely chopped
250g/9oz fresh pumpkin or butternut squash, peeled and roughly chopped
30ml/2 tbsp chopped fresh rosemary
250g/9oz/1½ cups risotto rice, preferably Arborio or Vialone Nano
about 750ml/1¼ pints/3 cups hot chicken stock, preferably fresh
50g/2oz/⅔ cup freshly grated Parmesan cheese, plus extra to serve
salt and ground black pepper

Melt half the butter in a heavy pan, add the onion and garlic, and cook for 10 minutes until softening. Add the chilli and cook for about 1 minute. Add the pumpkin or squash and cook, stirring constantly, for 5 minutes. Stir in the rosemary.

Add the rice, and stir with a wooden spoon to coat with the oil and vegetables. Cook for 2–3 minutes to toast the rice grains.

Begin to add the stock, a large ladleful at a time, stirring all the time until each ladleful has been absorbed into the rice. The rice should always be bubbling slowly. If not, add some more stock. Continue adding the stock like this, until the rice is tender and creamy, but the grains remain firm, and the pumpkin is beginning to disintegrate. (This should take about 20 minutes, depending on the type of rice used.) Taste and season well with salt and pepper.

Stir the remaining butter and the Parmesan cheese into the rice. Cover and let the risotto rest for 2–3 minutes, then serve straight away with extra Parmesan cheese.

Energy 585Kcal/2441kJ; Protein 14.4g; Carbohydrate 87.3g, of which sugars 5.7g; Fat 15.9g, of which saturates 3.5g; Cholesterol 8mg; Calcium 196mg; Fibre 3.2g; Sodium 151mg.

CHILLIES RELLENOS

Stuffed chillies are popular all over Mexico. The type of chilli used differs from region to region.
Poblanos and anaheims are quite mild, but you can use hotter chillies if you prefer.

Serves 6

46 fresh poblano or Anaheim
   chillies
2 potatoes, total weight about
   400g/14oz
200g/7oz/scant 1 cup cream
   cheese
200g/7oz/1¾ cups grated
   mature (sharp) Cheddar
   cheese
5ml/1 tsp salt
2.5ml/½ tsp ground black
   pepper
2 eggs, separated
115g/4oz/1 cup plain (all-
   purpose) flour
2.5ml/½ tsp white pepper
oil, for frying
chilli flakes, to garnish
   (optional)

Cut a slit down one side of each chilli. Dry-fry the chillies in a pan, turning frequently, until they blister. Place in a plastic bag and tie the top to keep the steam in. Set aside for 20 minutes, then peel off the skins and remove the seeds through the slits, keeping the chillies whole. Dry with kitchen paper and set aside.

Peel the potatoes and cut them into small dice. Bring a pan of water to the boil, add the potatoes and return to the boil. Lower the heat and simmer for 5 minutes, or until the potatoes are just tender, and drain.

Put the cream cheese in a bowl with the mature cheese. Add 2.5ml/ ½ tsp of the salt and the black pepper. Mix in the potato. Spoon potato filling into each chilli. Put them on a plate, cover with clear film (plastic wrap) and chill for 1 hour to firm up.

Put the egg whites in a clean, grease-free bowl and whisk to firm peaks. In another bowl, beat the yolks until pale, then fold in the whites. Scrape the mixture into a large, shallow dish. Spread out the flour in another shallow dish and season it with the remaining salt and the white pepper.

Heat the oil for deep-frying to 190°C/375°F. Coat a few chillies first in flour and then in egg before frying the chillies in batches until golden and crisp. Drain on kitchen paper and serve hot, garnished with a sprinkle of chilli flakes for extra heat, if desired.

Energy 498kcal/2072kJ; Protein 14.9g;
Carbohydrate 27.8g, of which sugars 32g;
Fat 26.5g, of which saturates 18.6g;
Cholesterol 127mg; Calcium 322mg;
Fibre 1.8g; Sodium 374mg

HERB AND CHILLI AUBERGINES

Plump and juicy aubergines (eggplant) are delicious steamed until tender and then tossed in a fragrant chilli and mint dressing with crunchy water chestnuts.

Serves 4

*500g/1¼lb firm, baby
   aubergines (eggplants)*
30ml/2 tbsp sunflower oil
*6 garlic cloves, very finely
   chopped*
*15ml/1 tbsp very finely chopped
   fresh root ginger*
*8 spring onions (scallions), cut
   diagonally into 2.5cm/1in
   lengths*
*2 red chillies, seeded and thinly
   sliced*
45ml/3 tbsp light soy sauce
15ml/1 tbsp Chinese rice wine
*15ml/1 tbsp golden caster
   (superfine) sugar or palm
   sugar*
a large handful of mint leaves
*30–45ml/2–3 tbsp chopped
   coriander (cilantro) leaves*
*115g/4oz water chestnuts,
   chopped*
*50g/2oz roasted peanuts,
   chopped*
*steamed egg noodles or rice,
   to serve*

Cut the aubergines in half lengthways and place on a heatproof plate.

Place a steamer rack in a wok and add 5cm/2in of water. Bring the water to the boil and lower the plate on to the rack and reduce the heat to low. Cover and steam the aubergines for 25–30 minutes, until they are cooked through. (Check the water level regularly, adding more if necessary.) Set aside the aubergines to cool.

Place the oil in a clean, dry wok and place over a medium heat. When hot, add the garlic, ginger, spring onions and chillies and stir-fry for 2–3 minutes. Remove from the heat and stir in the soy sauce, rice wine and sugar.

Add the mint leaves, chopped coriander, water chestnuts and peanuts to the aubergine and toss. Pour the garlic-ginger mixture evenly over the vegetables, toss gently and serve with steamed egg noodles or rice.

Energy 177Kcal/739kJ; Protein 6.2g; Carbohydrate 12.1g, of which sugars 9g; Fat 12g, of which saturates 1.9g; Cholesterol 0mg; Calcium 46mg; Fibre 4.4g; Sodium 823mg.

THAI ASPARAGUS WITH CHILLI AND GINGER

This is an excitingly different way of cooking asparagus. The crunchy texture is retained and the flavour is complemented by the addition of galangal and chilli.

Serves 2–4

350g/12oz asparagus stalks
30ml/2 tbsp vegetable oil
1 garlic clove, crushed
15ml/1 tbsp sesame seeds,
    toasted
2.5cm/1in piece fresh galangal,
    finely shredded
1 fresh red chilli, seeded and
    finely chopped
15ml/1 tbsp Thai fish sauce
15ml/1 tbsp light soy sauce
45ml/3 tbsp water
5ml/1 tsp light brown sugar

Heat the oil in a wok and stir-fry the garlic, sesame seeds and galangal for 3–4 seconds. Do not allow to brown but cook until the garlic is just beginning to turn golden.

Add the asparagus and chilli to the pan. Cook for 1 minute, stirring constantly, then add the fish sauce, soy sauce, water and sugar.

Toss over the heat for a further 2 minutes, or until the asparagus just begins to soften. Serve on warmed serving dishes.

Energy 120Kcal/492kJ; Protein 4.1g;
Carbohydrate 2.4g, of which sugars 23g;
Fat 10.4g, of which saturates 1.4g;
Cholesterol 0mg; Calcium 75mg;
Fibre 2.1g; Sodium 537mg

PATATAS BRAVAS

There are several variations on this chilli and potato dish, but the most important thing is the spicing, which is made hotter still by adding vinegar.

Serves 4

675g/1½lb small new potatoes
75ml/5 tbsp olive oil
2 garlic cloves, sliced
3 dried chillies, seeded
*   and chopped*
2.5ml/½ tsp ground cumin
10ml/2 tsp paprika
30ml/2 tbsp red or white
*   wine vinegar*
1 red or green (bell) pepper,
*   seeded and sliced*
coarse sea salt, for sprinkling
*   (optional)*

Energy 256kcal/1070kJ; Protein 3.3g;
Carbohydrate 30g, of which sugars 4.9g;
Fat 14.4g, of which saturates 2.2g;
Cholesterol 0mg; Calcium 14mg;
Fibre 2.4g; Sodium 20mg

Scrub the potatoes and put them into a pan of salted water. Bring to the boil and cook for 10 minutes, or until almost tender. Drain and leave to cool slightly. Peel, if you like, then cut into chunks.

Heat the oil in a large frying or sauté pan and fry the potatoes, turning them frequently, until golden.

Meanwhile, crush together the garlic, chillies and cumin using a mortar and pestle. Mix the paste with the paprika and wine vinegar, then add to the potatoes with the sliced pepper and cook, stirring, for 2 minutes. Scatter with salt, if using, and serve hot as a tapas dish or cold as a side dish.

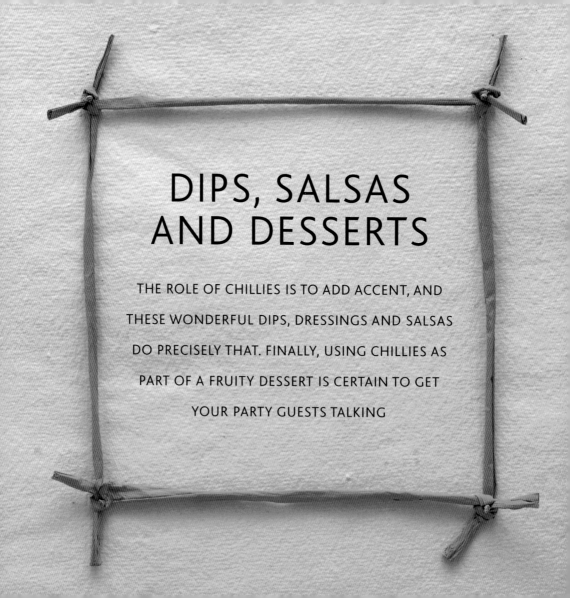

DIPS, SALSAS AND DESSERTS

THE ROLE OF CHILLIES IS TO ADD ACCENT, AND
THESE WONDERFUL DIPS, DRESSINGS AND SALSAS
DO PRECISELY THAT. FINALLY, USING CHILLIES AS
PART OF A FRUITY DESSERT IS CERTAIN TO GET
YOUR PARTY GUESTS TALKING

SAMBAL SERONDENG

A quintessential dressing in Malaysia and Singapore, serondeng is delicious sprinkled over dishes like beef rendang, coconut milk kormas and curries, or over plain rice as a relish.

Serves 6–8
2 stalks lemon grass
5 shallots
4 garlic cloves
3 fresh red chillies, seeded
50g/2oz tempeh (fermented soy bean cake)
30ml/2 tbsp vegetable or groundnut (peanut) oil
175g/6oz fresh coconut, grated or 100g/3½oz desiccated (dry, unsweetened, shredded) coconut
2.5ml/½ tsp salt
2.5ml/½ tsp sugar

Energy 120Kcal/494kJ; Protein 1.7g;
Carbohydrate 4.1g, of which sugars 3.3g;
Fat 10.8g, of which saturates 7g;
Cholesterol 0mg; Calcium 44mg;
Fibre 2.2g; Sodium 128mg.

Trim the lemon grass stalks and slice the 7.5cm/3in at the root end into very thin rounds. Peel and slice the shallots and the garlic. Slice the chillies diagonally into thin pieces.

Cut the tempeh into small dice, and fry it in oil in a wok or heavy pan until light brown. Crush it coarsely.

Heat another wok without oil and dry fry the lemon grass, shallots, garlic and chillies until just sizzled. Add the coconut, and stir-fry with a to and fro motion until all the ingredients are golden brown.

Add the crushed tempeh, salt and sugar and fry, stirring, until well-mixed. Remove from the heat and leave to cool before storing in an air-tight container, if not serving immediately. Keep the serondeng in the refrigerator and eat within a week.

LIME AND CHILLI DIP

For this Malay dip, sambal limau, it is essential to use limes that have very thin skins that can be grated very thinly to add to the sauce, otherwise the sauce will have a bitter edge.

Serves 4–6

6 calamansi limes
4 red chillies, deseeded
2 garlic cloves
2 spring onions (scallions)
2 kaffir lime leaves
5ml/1 tsp sugar
15ml/1 tbsp fish sauce
30ml/2 tbsp water

Finely grate the rind (zest) of one lime into a bowl. Squeeze the juice from all the limes into the bowl and, with a spoon, scoop out the flesh. Discard the seeds.

Finely chop the chillies, garlic and spring onions. Shred the lime leaves finely. Mix these ingredients into the lime juice and add the sugar, fish sauce and water. Stir everything together.

Taste and adjust the proportions if necessary, adding more water or lime juice as needed. Serve the dip with fish and chicken dishes or salads.

COOK'S TIP
Calamansi (also called kesturi) limes have the thinnest skins. They are occasionally available in Thai and Filipino markets.

Energy 9Kcal/38kJ; Protein 0.6g; Carbohydrate 1.6g, of which sugars 1.3g; Fat 0.1g, of which saturates 0g; Cholesterol 0mg; Calcium 6mg; Fibre 0.1g; Sodium 179mg.

CHILLI, GARLIC AND GINGER SAUCE

Regarded as the holy trinity of spices, chillies, garlic and ginger have an extraordinary affinity when they are combined in the correct proportions.

Serves 4–6

10 fresh red chillies
10 cloves garlic
50g/2oz fresh root ginger
200ml/7fl oz/scant 1 cup rice
    wine vinegar
2.5ml/½ tsp salt
2.5ml/½ tsp sugar
30ml/2 tbsp vegetable oil
2 spring onions (scallions)

COOK'S TIP
After washing, the chillies
should be completely dry.
It is important that you
do not introduce moisture
into the sauce as it will
encourage bacterial growth
and the sauce will not
keep well.

Energy 339Kcal/1405kJ; Protein 13.9g;
Carbohydrate 18.1g, of which sugars 3.5g;
Fat 23.9g, of which saturates 2.7g;
Cholesterol 0mg; Calcium 100mg;
Fibre 4.6g; Sodium 1070mg.

Wash the chillies and pat them completely dry. Chop roughly without removing the seeds.

Peel the garlic and wipe dry with kitchen paper. Roughly chop.

With a sharp paring knife, peel or scrape off the thin outer skin of the ginger. Roughly chop the ginger.

Place all three ingredients in a mortar and pestle or food processor and process until fine, but be careful not to reduce it to a purée consistency. To facilitate the grinding, add a spoonful of the vinegar.

Turn the mixture into a bowl and combine with the remaining vinegar and the salt and sugar. Heat the oil in a small pan or wok and add to the sauce. Finely chop the spring onions and mix them in well. Keep in a jar with a screw-top lid for up to a week.

GUAJILLO CHILLI SALSA

This salsa can be served with enchiladas or steamed vegetables. It is also good with meats such as pork, and a little makes a fine seasoning for soups or stews.

Serves 4

2 tomatoes, total weight about
  200g/7oz
2 red (bell) peppers, cored,
  seeded and quartered
3 garlic cloves, in their skins
2 ancho chillies
2 guajillo chillies
30ml/2 tbsp tomato purée
  (paste)
5ml/1 tsp dried oregano
5ml/1 tsp soft dark brown sugar
300ml/½ pint/1¼ cups chicken
  stock

COOK'S TIP
Made from dried chillies,
this salsa has a well
rounded, fruity flavour
and is not too hot.

Preheat the oven to 200°C/400°F/Gas 6. Cut the tomatoes into quarters and place them in a roasting tin with the peppers and whole garlic cloves. Roast for 45 minutes–1 hour, until the tomatoes and peppers are slightly charred and the garlic has softened.

Put the peppers in a strong plastic bag and tie the top to keep the steam in. Set aside for 20 minutes. Remove the skin from the tomatoes. Meanwhile, soak the chillies in boiling water for 15 minutes until soft.

Remove the peppers from the bag and rub off the skins. Cut them in half, remove the cores and seeds, then chop the flesh roughly and put it in a food processor or blender. Drain the chillies, remove the stalks, then slit them and scrape out the seeds with a sharp knife. Chop the chillies roughly and add them to the peppers.

Add the roasted tomatoes to the food processor or blender. Squeeze the roasted garlic out of the skins and add to the tomato mixture, with the tomato purée, oregano, brown sugar and stock. Process until smooth.

Pour the mixture into a saucepan, place over a moderate heat and bring to the boil. Lower the heat and simmer for 10–15 minutes until the sauce has reduced to about half. Transfer to a bowl and serve immediately or, if serving cold, cover, leave to cool, then chill until required. The sauce will keep in the refrigerator for up to a week.

Energy 55kcal/230kJ; Protein 2.4g; Carbohydrate 10.4g, of which sugars 9.4g; Fat 0.6g, of which saturates 0.2g; Cholesterol 0mg; Calcium 19mg; Fibre 2.3g; Sodium 27mg

CHARGRILLED PINEAPPLE WITH CHILLI GRANITA

This is a bold dessert; attractive too, if you leave the green tops on the pineapple. Heating pineapple really brings the flavour to the fore and, with the ice-cold granita, it's the ideal finish to a barbecue.

Serves 8
2 medium, fresh pineapples
15ml/1 tbsp caster (superfine)
    sugar

For the granita
15ml/1 tbsp sugar
1 fresh long mild red chilli,
    seeded and finely chopped
900ml/1½ pints/3¾ cups
    pineapple juice or fresh purée

COOK'S TIP
If the granita has been in the freezer a long time, thaw for about 10 minutes in the refrigerator before serving and fork it over to break up the ice crystals.

To make the granita, place the sugar and chilli in a small heavy pan with 30ml/2 tbsp of the pineapple juice. Heat gently until the sugar has dissolved, then bring to a fast boil for 30 seconds. Pour the remaining pineapple juice into a shallow freezerproof container. Stir in the chilli mixture and freeze for 2 hours. Fork the frozen edges of the sorbet mixture into the centre and freeze for a further 1½ hours until crunchy. Give it another fork over. Return it to the freezer until ready to use (it will keep for up to 1 week).

Cut each pineapple lengthways into four equal wedges. Mix the sugar and 15ml/1 tbsp water in a small bowl. Heat the griddle over a high heat. Lower the heat slightly. Brush the cut sides of the pineapple wedges with the sugar mixture and grill for about 1 minute on each side, or until branded with grill marks. Serve warm with the granita.

Energy 112kcal/482kJ; Protein 0.9g;
Carbohydrate 28.4g, of which sugars
28.4g; Fat 0.4g, of which saturates 0g;
Cholesterol 0mg; Calcium 34mg;
Fibre 1.5g; Sodium 12mg.

CHILLI SORBET

Served during or after dinner this unusual but refreshing sorbet is sure to become a talking point. Use a medium-chilli rather than any of the really fiery varieties.

Serves 6

1 fresh red chilli
finely grated rind (zest) and juice
*   of 2 lemons*
finely grated rind (zest) and juice
*   of 2 limes*
225g/8oz/1 cup caster
*   (superfine) sugar*
750ml/1¼ pints/3 cups water
pared lemon or lime rind (zest),
*   to decorate*

COOK'S TIP
For an added kick, drizzle with tequila or vodka before serving. To avoid getting chilli juice on your skin wash your hands after dealing with them.

Energy 150kcal/640kJ; Protein 0.5g; Carbohydrate 39.4g, of which sugars 39.4g; Fat 0.1g, of which saturates 0g; Cholesterol 0mg; Calcium 23mg; Fibre 0g; Sodium 3mg.

Cut the chilli in half, removing all the seeds and any pith with a small sharp knife, and then chop the flesh very finely.

Put the chilli, lemon and lime rind, sugar and water in a heavy-based saucepan. Heat gently and stir while the sugar dissolves. Bring to the boil, then simmer for 2 minutes without stirring. Let cool.

Add lemon and lime juice to the chilli syrup and chill until very cold.

By hand: Pour the mixture into a container and freeze for 3–4 hours, beating twice as it thickens. Return to the freezer until ready to serve.

Using an ice cream maker: Churn the mixture until it holds its shape. Scrape into a container and freeze until ready to serve.

Spoon into glasses and decorate with the lemon or lime rind.

INDEX

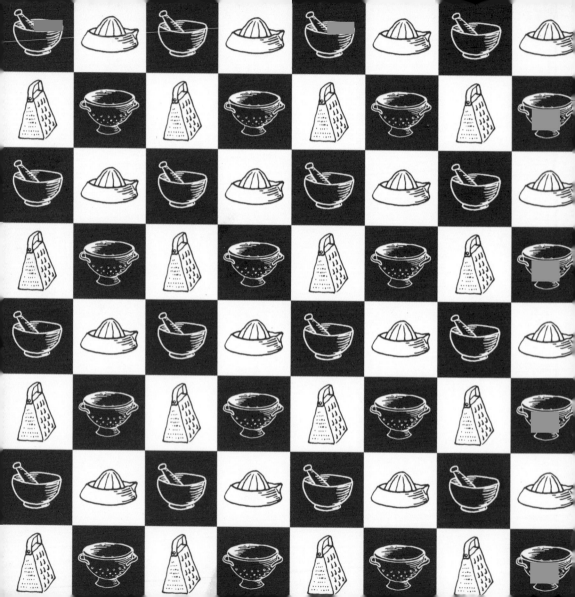